A Divine and Supernatural Light

A DIVINE AND SUPERNATURAL LIGHT

IMMEDIATELY IMPARTED TO THE SOUL BY
THE SPIRIT OF GOD, SHOWN TO BE BOTH A
SCRIPTURAL AND RATIONAL DOCTRINE,

In a sermon preached at *Northampton*, and
published at the desire of some of the hearers.

JONATHAN EDWARDS, A.M.

Late pastor of the church in *Northampton,* Massachusetts.

CURIOSMITH

MINNEAPOLIS

2012

Published by Curiosmith.
P. O. Box 390293, Minneapolis, Minnesota, 55439.
Internet: curiosmith.com.
E-mail: shopkeeper@curiosmith.com.

Previously printed by Samuel Kneeland and Timothy Green in Boston in 1734.

The text of this edition is from *Works of Jonathan Edwards,* edited by Edward Hickman, 1843.

The Outline of the Contents was added to this edition by the publisher.

ISBN 9781935626633

OUTLINE OF THE CONTENTS

———◆◇◆———

Christ says as he does *to* Peter and *of* Peter in the text:
1. That Peter is pronounced blessed. (PAGE 8.)
2. That God, and he only, had revealed it to him. (PAGE 8.)
    First, How peculiarly favored he was of God above others.
    Secondly, This knowledge is above any that flesh and blood can reveal.

DOCTRINE (PAGE 10.)
I. Show what this divine light is. (PAGE 11.)
    First, in a few things what it is not. (PAGE 11.)
        1. Not those convictions that natural men may have of their sin and misery.
        2. Not any impression made upon the imagination.
        3. Not any new truths or propositions not contained in the word of God.
        4. Not every affecting view that men have of religious things.
    Secondly, Positively what this spiritual and divine light is. (PAGE 15.)
        1. A true sense of the divine excellency of the things of religion.
        2. A conviction of the truth and reality of them.
            First, Indirectly, and that two ways.
                1. The mind becomes susceptive of the due force of rational arguments for their truth.
                2. It not only removes the hindrances of reason, but positively helps reason.
            Secondly, The excellency of these things is so superlative.
II. The light is given immediately by God, and not obtained by natural means. (PAGE 20.)
    1. It is not intended that the natural faculties are not used in it. (PAGE 21.)
    2. It is not intended that outward means have no concern in this affair. (PAGE 22.)
    3. It does not use of any means that operate by their own power. (PAGE 22.)

(Outline of the Contents is continued on the next page.)

A DIVINE AND SUPERNATURAL LIGHT

IMMEDIATELY IMPARTED TO THE SOUL BY
THE SPIRIT OF GOD, SHOWN TO BE BOTH
A SCRIPTURAL AND RATIONAL DOCTRINE[1]

A SERMON BY

JONATHAN EDWARDS, A.M.

And Jesus answered and said unto him, Blessed art thou, Simon Bar-jona: for flesh and blood hath not revealed it unto thee, but my Father which is in heaven.—MATTHEW 16:17.

C hrist addresses these words to Peter upon occasion of his professing his faith in him as the Son of God. Our Lord was inquiring of his disciples, whom men said that he was; not that he needed to be informed, but only to introduce and give occasion to what follows. They answer, that some said he was John the Baptist, and some Elias, and others Jeremias, or one of the prophets. When they had thus given an account whom others said that

---

1 Preached at *Northampton*, and published at the desire of some of the hearers.

he was, Christ asks them, whom they said that he was? Simon Peter, whom we find always zealous and forward, was the first to answer: he readily replied to the question, *Thou art Christ, the Son of the living God.*

Upon this occasion, Christ says as he does *to* him and *of* him in the text: in which we may observe,

1. That Peter is pronounced blessed on this account.—*Blessed art thou*—"Thou art a happy man, that thou art not ignorant of this, that I am *Christ, the Son of the living God.* Thou art distinguishingly happy. Others are blinded, and have dark and deluded apprehensions, as you have now given an account, some thinking that I am Elias, and some that I am Jeremias, and some one thing, and some another; but none of them thinking right, all of them misled. Happy art thou, that art so distinguished as to know the truth in this matter."

2. The evidence of this his happiness declared; *viz.* That God, and he *only*, had *revealed it* to him. This is an evidence of his being *blessed,*

First, As it shows how peculiarly favoured he was of God above others: *q.d.* "How highly favored art thou, that others, wise and great men, the scribes, Pharisees, and Rulers, and the nation in general, are left in darkness, to follow their own misguided apprehensions; and that thou shouldst be singled out, as it were, by name, that my heavenly Father should thus set his love on *thee, Simon Bar-jona.*—This argues thee *blessed,* that thou shouldst thus be the object of God's distinguishing love."

Secondly, it evidences his blessedness also, as it intimates that this knowledge is above any that *flesh* and *blood* can *reveal*. "This is such knowledge as only my *Father which is in heaven* can give: it is too high and excellent to be communicated by such means as other knowledge is. Thou art *blessed*, that thou knowest what God alone can teach thee."

The original of this knowledge is here declared, both negatively and positively. *Positively*, as God is here declared the author of it. *Negatively*, as it is declared, that *flesh and blood had not revealed it*. God is the author of all knowledge and understanding whatsoever. He is the author of all moral prudence, and of the skill that men have in their secular business. Thus it is said of all in Israel that were *wise-hearted*, and skilled in embroidering, that God had *filled* them *with the spirit of wisdom*. Exodus 28:3.

God is the author of such knowledge; yet so that *flesh and blood reveals it*. Mortal men are capable of imparting the knowledge of human arts and sciences, and skill in temporal affairs. God is the author of such knowledge by those means: *flesh and blood* is employed as the *mediate* or *second* cause of it: he conveys it by the power and influence of natural means. But this spiritual knowledge spoken of in the text, is what God is the author of, and none else: he *reveals it*, and *flesh and blood reveals it not*. He imparts this knowledge immediately, not making use of any intermediate natural causes, as he does in other knowledge.

What had passed in the preceding discourse naturally occasioned Christ to observe this; because the disciples had been telling how others did not know him, but were generally mistaken about him, divided and confounded in their opinions of him: but Peter had declared his assured faith, that he was the *Son of God*. Now it was natural to observe, how it was not *flesh and blood* that had *revealed it to him*, but God; for if this knowledge were dependent on natural causes or means, how came it to pass that they, a company of poor fishermen, illiterate men, and persons of low education, attained to the knowledge of the truth; while the scribes and Pharisees, men of vastly higher advantages, and greater knowledge and sagacity in other matters, remained in ignorance? This could be owing only to the gracious distinguishing influence and revelation of the Spirit of God. Hence, what I would make the subject of my present discourse from these words, is this

DOCTRINE

That there is such a thing as a spiritual and divine light, immediately imparted to the soul by God, of a different nature from any that is obtained by natural means.—And on this subject I would,

    I. Show what this divine light is.
    II. How it is given immediately by God, and not obtained by natural means.
    III. Show the truth of the doctrine.
   And then conclude with a brief improvement.

I. I would show what this spiritual and divine light is. And in order to it, would show,

First, in a few things what it is not. And here,

1. Those convictions that natural men may have of their sin and misery, is not this spiritual and divine light. Men in a natural condition may have convictions of the guilt that lies upon them, and of the anger of God, and their danger of divine vengeance. Such convictions are from the light of truth. That some sinners have a greater conviction of their guilt and misery than others, is because some have more light, or more of an apprehension of truth, than others. And this light and conviction may be from the Spirit of God; the Spirit convinces men of sin: but yet nature is much more concerned in it than in the communication of that spiritual and divine light that is spoken of in the doctrine; it is from the Spirit of God only as assisting natural principles, and not as infusing any new principles. Common grace differs from special, in that it influences only by assisting of nature; and not by imparting grace, or bestowing any thing above nature. The light that is obtained is wholly natural, or of no superior kind to what mere nature attains to, though more of that kind be obtained than would be obtained if men were left wholly to themselves: or, in other words, common grace only assists the faculties of the soul to do that more fully which they do by nature, as natural conscience or reason will by mere nature make a man sensible of guilt, and will accuse and condemn him when he has done amiss. Conscience is a principle natural to men; and the work that it doth

naturally, or of itself, is to give an apprehension of right and wrong, and to suggest to the mind the relation that there is between right and wrong and a retribution. The Spirit of God, in those convictions which unregenerate men sometimes have, assists conscience to do this work in a further degree than it would do if they were left to themselves. He helps it against those things that tend to stupify it, and obstruct its exercise. But in the renewing and sanctifying work of the Holy Ghost, those things are wrought in the soul that are above nature, and of which there is nothing of the like kind in the soul by nature; and they are caused to exist in the soul habitually, and according to such a stated constitution or law that lays such a foundation for exercises in a continued course as is called a principle of nature. Not only are remaining principles assisted to do their work more freely and fully, but those principles are restored that were utterly destroyed by the fall; and the mind thenceforward habitually exerts those acts that the dominion of sin had made it as wholly destitute of as a dead body is of vital acts.

The Spirit of God acts in a very different manner in the one case, from what he doth in the other. He may indeed act upon the mind of a natural man, but he acts in the mind of a saint as an indwelling vital principle. He acts upon the mind of an unregenerate person as an extrinsic occasional agent; for in acting upon them, he doth not unite himself to them; for notwithstanding all his influences that they may possess, they are still sensual, having not the Spirit. Jude 19. But he unites himself with the mind of a saint, takes him for his temple, actuates and influences him as a new supernatural principle of life and action. There is this difference, that the Spirit of God, in acting in the soul of a godly man, exerts and communicates himself there in his own proper nature. Holiness is the proper nature of the Spirit of God. The Holy Spirit operates in the minds of the godly, by uniting himself to them, and living in them, exerting his own nature in the exercise of their faculties. The Spirit of God may act upon a creature, and yet not in acting communicate himself. The Spirit of God may act upon inanimate creatures; as, *the Spirit moved upon the face of the waters*, in the beginning of creation; so the Spirit of God may act upon the minds of men many ways, and communicate himself no more than when he acts upon an inanimate creature. For instance, he may excite thoughts in them, may assist their natural reason and understanding, or may assist other natural principles, and this without any union with the soul, but may act, as it were, upon an external object. But as he acts in his holy influences and spiritual operations, he acts in a way of peculiar communication of himself; so that the subject is thence denominated spiritual.

2. This spiritual and divine light does not consist in any impression made upon the imagination. It is no impression upon the mind, as though one saw anything with the bodily eyes. It is no imagination or idea of an outward light or glory, or any beauty of form or countenance, or a visible lustre or brightness of any object. The imagination may be strongly impressed with such things;

but this is not spiritual light. Indeed when the mind has a lively discovery of spiritual things, and is greatly affected by the power of divine light, it may, and probably very commonly doth, much affect the imagination; so that impressions of an outward beauty or brightness may *accompany* those spiritual discoveries. But spiritual light is not that impression upon the imagination, but an exceedingly different thing. Natural men may have lively impressions on their imaginations; and we cannot determine but that the devil, who transforms himself into an angel of light, may cause imaginations of an outward beauty, or visible glory, and of sounds and speeches, and other such things; but these are things of a vastly inferior nature to spiritual light.

3. This spiritual light is not the suggesting of any new truths or propositions not contained in the word of God. This suggesting of new truths or doctrines to the mind, independent of any antecedent revelation of those propositions, either in word or writing, is inspiration; such as the prophets and apostles had, and such as some enthusiasts pretend to. But this spiritual light that I am speaking of, is quite a different thing than inspiration. It reveals no new doctrine, it suggests no new proposition to the mind, it teaches no new thing of God, or Christ, or another world, not taught in the Bible, but only gives a due apprehension of those things that are taught in the word of God.

4. It is not every affecting view that men have of religious things that is this spiritual and divine light. Men

by mere principles of nature are capable of being affected with things that have a special relation to religion as well as other things. A person by mere nature, for instance, may be liable to be affected with the story of Jesus Christ, and the sufferings he underwent, as well as by any other tragic story. He may be the more affected with it from the interest he conceives mankind to have in it. Yea, he may be affected with it without believing it; as well as a man may be affected with what he reads in a romance, or sees acted in a stage-play. He may be affected with a lively and eloquent description of many pleasant things that attend the state of the blessed in heaven, as well as his imagination be entertained by romantic description of the pleasantness of fairy land, or the like. And a common belief of the truth of such things, from education or otherwise, may help forward their affection. We read in Scripture of many that were greatly affected with things of a religious nature, who yet are there represented as wholly graceless, and many of them very ill men. A person therefore may have affecting views of the things of religion, and yet be very destitute of spiritual light. Flesh and blood may be the author of this: one man may give another an affecting view of divine things with but common assistance; but God alone can give a spiritual discovery of them.—But I proceed to show,

Secondly, Positively what this spiritual and divine light is.

And it may be thus described: A true sense of the divine excellency of the things revealed in the word of God, and a conviction of the truth and reality of them thence arising. This spiritual light primarily consists in the former of these, *viz.* A real sense and apprehension of the divine excellency of things revealed in the word of God. A spiritual and saving conviction of the truth and reality of these things, arises from such a sight of their divine excellency and glory; so that this conviction of their truth is an effect and natural consequence of this sight of their divine glory. There is therefore in the spiritual light,

1. A true sense of the divine and superlative excellency of the things of religion; a real sense of the excellency of God and Jesus Christ, and of the work of redemption, and the ways and works of God revealed in the gospel. There is a divine and superlative glory in these things; an excellency that is of a vastly higher kind, and more sublime nature, than in other things; a glory greatly distinguishing them from all that is earthly and temporal. He that is spiritually enlightened truly apprehends and sees it, or has a sense of it. He does not merely rationally believe that God is glorious, but he has a sense of the gloriousness of God in his heart. There is not only a rational belief that God is holy, and that holiness is a good thing, but there is a sense of the loveliness of God's holiness. There is not only a speculatively judging that God is gracious, but a sense how amiable God is on account of the beauty of this divine attribute.

There is a twofold knowledge of good of which God has made the mind of man capable. The first, that which is merely notional; as when a person only speculatively judges that any thing is, which, by the agreement of mankind, is called good or excellent, *viz.* that which is most to general advantage, and between which and a reward there is a suitableness,—and the like. And the other thing is, that which consists in the sense of the heart; as when the heart is sensible of pleasure and delight in the presence of the idea of it. In the former is exercised merely the speculative faculty, or the understanding, in distinction from the will or the disposition of the soul. In the latter, the will, or inclination, or heart are mainly concerned.

Thus there is a difference between having an *opinion*, that God is holy and gracious, and having a *sense* of the loveliness and beauty of that holiness and grace. There is a difference between having a rational judgment that honey is sweet, and having a sense of its sweetness. A man may have the former that knows not how honey tastes; but a man cannot have the latter unless he has an idea of the taste of honey in his mind. So there is a difference between believing that a person is beautiful, and having a sense of his beauty. The former may be obtained by hearsay, but the latter only by seeing the countenance. When the heart is sensible of the beauty and amiableness of a thing, it necessarily feels pleasure in the apprehension. It is implied in a person's being heartily sensible of the loveliness of a thing, that the idea of it is pleasant to his soul; which is a far different thing from having a rational opinion that it is excellent.

2. There arises from this sense of the divine excellency of things contained in the word of God, a conviction of

the truth and reality of them; and that either indirectly or directly.

First, Indirectly, and that two ways.

1. As the prejudices of the heart, against the truth of divine things, are hereby removed; so that the mind becomes susceptive of the due force of rational arguments for their truth. The mind of man is naturally full of prejudices against divine truth. It is full of enmity against the doctrines of the gospel; which is a disadvantage to those arguments that prove their truth, and causes them to lose their force upon the mind. But when a person has discovered to him the divine excellency of Christian doctrines, this destroys the enmity, removes those prejudices, sanctifies the reason, and causes it to lie open to the force of arguments for their truth.

Hence was the different effect that Christ's miracles had to convince the disciples, from what they had to convince the scribes and Pharisees. Not that they had a stronger reason, or had their reason more improved; but their reason was sanctified, and those blinding prejudices, that the scribes and Pharisees were under, were removed by the sense they had of the excellency of Christ, and his doctrine.

2. It not only removes the hindrances of reason, but positively helps reason. It makes even the speculative notions more lively. It engages the attention of the mind, with more fixedness and intenseness to that kind of objects; which causes it to have a clearer view of them, and enables it more clearly to see their mutual relations,

and occasions it to take more notice of them. The ideas themselves that otherwise are dim and obscure, are by this means impressed with the greater strength, and have a light cast upon them; so that the mind can better judge of them. As he that beholds objects on the face of the earth, when the light of the sun is cast upon them, is under greater advantage to discern them in their true forms and natural relations, than he that sees them in a dim twilight.

The mind being sensible of the excellency of divine objects, dwells upon them with delight; and the powers of the soul are more awakened and enlivened to employ themselves in the contemplation of them, and exert themselves more fully and much more to purpose. The beauty of the objects draws on the faculties, and draws forth their exercises; so that reason itself is under far greater advantages for its proper and free exercises, and to attain its proper end, free of the darkness and delusion.—But,

Secondly, A true sense of the divine excellency of the things of God's word doth more directly and immediately convince us of their truth; and that because the excellency of these things is so superlative. There is a beauty in them so divine and God-like, that it greatly and evidently distinguishes them from things merely human, or that of which men are the inventors and authors; a glory so high and great, that when clearly seen, commands assent to their divine reality. When there is an actual and lively discovery of this beauty and excellency, it will not allow of any such thought as that it is the fruit of men's invention. This is a kind of intuitive and immediate evidence. They believe the doctrines of God's word to be divine, because they see a divine, and transcendent, and most evidently distinguishing glory in them; such a glory as, if clearly seen, does not leave room to doubt of their being of God, and not of men.

Such a conviction of the truths of religion as this, arising from a sense of their divine excellency, is included in saving faith. And this original of it, is that by which it is most essentially distinguished from that common assent, of which unregenerate men are capable.

II. I proceed now to the *second* thing proposed, *viz.* To show how this light is immediately given by God, and not obtained by natural means.[2] And here,

2 In the preceding statement and the following explanation, our author might have rendered the subject of "divine light immediately imparted to the soul" more perspicuous, by a fuller use of that *analogy* which the Scripture holds forth, between the common theory of vision and the doctrine he defends. Let the remarks which follow be candidly considered.

1. In the sacred Scriptures, God is represented as "the Father of lights," and Christ as "the Sun of righteousness." Yea, it is asserted, that "God is LIGHT," and that he "shines into the heart." These and similar expressions, with which the Old and New Testament abound, show that there is a strong analogy between the light in the natural world, and something spiritual that is expressed by the same term.

2. As the light of day proceeds from the natural sun, and shines into the eye; so the spiritual or supernatural light proceeds from God, and shines into the heart, or *mind*. Thus the analogy holds, not only as to the *things* intended—in their sources, and their emanations—but also as to the *organs* of reception.

3. The *existence* of light in the eye depends neither on the *perception* of it, nor on any external *object*. Our *perception* of illuminated objects is the *effect* of light's existence in the organ of vision. Without light both in the eye, and on the object to be seen, there can be no perception of that object. In like manner, the existence of that light which

1. It is not intended that the natural faculties are not used in it. They are the subject of this light; and in such a manner, that they are not merely passive, but active in it. God, in letting in this light into the soul, deals with man according to his nature, and makes use of his rational faculties. But yet this light is not the less immediately from God for that; the faculties are made use of as the subject,

emanates from God, and shines into the mind, is there (that is, in the mind) prior to, and independent on the mental perception of it; and consequentially is there irrespective of the knowledge of objects to be known by it.—Therefore,

4. Knowledge can be called "light," only in a *secondary* sense, both naturally and spiritually; that is, by a metonymy, because it is the *effect* of light. We *know* a visible object, because we see it; and we see it, because light shines both on the object, and into the eye. It is by divine light shining into the mind that we have a spiritual knowledge of God, of Christ, or of any other object; in other words, a holy emanation or influence from God, called light, is the cause why any person or thing is known in a spiritual manner.

5. When any identify this divine *light*, these rays of the Sun of righteousness, with knowledge, (however spiritual and excellent,) because the latter is metonymically called "light," they are chargeable with identifying cause and effect, and therefore of confounding things which essentially differ. For spiritual *light*, in the primary and proper sense, emanates immediately from God, as rays from the sun; but this cannot be said of knowledge, because the perception of an object, which is our act, must intervene. Knowledge presupposes the primary light, and is also dependent on the objective truths perceived. All knowledge, whether natural or spiritual, stands essentially related to objects known; so that without those objects it can have no existence. The knowledge of objects to be seen, therefore, is the effect of *two causes* concurring, the object itself and light; whereas the "divine light which is immediately imparted to the soul," has but *one cause*, even the sovereign will of God.

6. *Coroll.* The theological notion which makes all spiritual light in man to consist in knowledge, and which is become too fashionable in the present day, is contrary to Scripture, and to rational analogy.—W.

and not as the cause. As the use we make of our eyes in beholding various objects, when the sun arises, is not the cause of the light that discovers those objects to us.

2. It is not intended that outward means have no concern in this affair. It is not in this affair, as in inspiration, where new truths are suggested: for by this light is given only a due apprehension of the same truths that are revealed in the word of God; and therefore it is not given without the word. The gospel is employed in this affair. This light is the "light of the glorious gospel of Christ," 2 Corinthians 4:4. The gospel is as a glass, by which this light is conveyed to us. 1 Corinthians 13:12. "Now we see through a glass."—But,

3. When it is said that this light is given immediately by God, and not obtained by natural means, hereby is intended, that it is given by God without making use of any means that operate by their own power or natural force. God makes use of means; but it is not as mediate causes to produce this effect. There are not truly any second causes of it; but it is produced by God immediately. The word of God is no proper cause of this effect; but is made use of only to convey to the mind the subject-matter of this saving instruction: and this indeed it doth convey to us by natural force or influence. It conveys to our minds these doctrines; it is the cause of a notion of them in our heads, but not of the sense of their divine excellency in our hearts. Indeed a person cannot have spiritual light without the word. But that does not argue, that the word properly causes that light. The mind cannot

see the excellency of any doctrine, unless that doctrine be first in the mind; but seeing the excellency of the doctrine may be immediately from the Spirit of God; though the conveying of the doctrine or proposition itself may be by the word. So that the notions which are the subject-matter of this light, are conveyed to the mind by the word of God; but that due sense of the heart, wherein this light formally consists, is immediately by the Spirit of God. As for instance, the notion that there is a Christ, and that Christ is holy and gracious, is conveyed to the mind by the word of God; but the sense of the excellency of Christ by reason of that holiness and grace, is nevertheless immediately the work of the Holy Spirit.—I come now,

III. To show the truth of the doctrine; that is, to show that there is such a thing as that spiritual light that has been described, thus immediately let into the mind by God. And here I would show briefly, that this doctrine is both *scriptural* and *rational*.

First, it is scriptural. My text is not only full to the purpose, but it is a doctrine with which the Scripture abounds. We are there abundantly taught, that the saints differ from the ungodly in this, that they have the knowledge of God, and a sight of God, and of Jesus Christ. I shall mention but few texts out of many: 1 John 3:6. "Whosoever sinneth, hath not seen him, nor known him." 3 John 11. "He that doeth good, is of God: but he that doeth evil, hath not seen God." John 14:19. "The world seeth me no more; but ye see me." John 17:3. "And this is eternal life, that they might know thee, the only true God, and Jesus Christ whom thou hast sent." This knowledge, or sight of God and Christ, cannot be a mere speculative knowledge; because it is spoken of as that wherein they differ from the ungodly. And by these scriptures it must not only be a different knowledge in degree and circumstances, and different in its effects; but it must be entirely different in nature and kind.

And this light and knowledge is always spoken of as immediately given of God; Matthew 11:25–27. "At that time Jesus answered and said, I thank thee, O Father, Lord of heaven and earth, because thou hast hid these things from the wise and prudent, and hast revealed them unto babes. Even so, Father, for so it seemed good in thy sight. All things are delivered unto me of my Father: and no man knoweth the Father, save the Son, and he to whomsoever the Son will reveal him." Here this effect is ascribed exclusively to the arbitrary operation and gift of God bestowing this knowledge on whom he will, and distinguishing those with it who have the least natural advantage or means for knowledge, even babes, when it is denied to the wise and prudent. And imparting this knowledge is here appropriated to the Son of God, as his sole prerogative. And again, 2 Corinthians 4:6. "For God who commanded the light to shine out of darkness, hath shined in our hearts, to give the light of the knowledge of the glory of God, in the face of Jesus Christ." This plainly shows, that there is a discovery of the divine superlative glory and excellency of God and Christ, peculiar to the saints; and also, that it is as immediately from God, as light from the sun: and that it is the immediate effect of his power and will. For it is compared to God's creating the light by his powerful word in the beginning of the creation; and is said to be by the Spirit of the Lord, in the 18th verse of the preceding chapter. God is spoken of as giving the knowledge of Christ in conversion, as of what before was hidden and unseen, Galatians 1:15, 16. "But when it pleased God, who separated me from my mother's womb, and called me by his grace, to reveal his Son in me."—The Scripture also speaks plainly of such a knowledge of the word of God, as has been described, as the immediate gift of God; Psalm 119:18. "Open thou mine eyes, that I may behold wondrous things out of thy law." What could the psalmist mean, when he begged of God to open his eyes? Was he ever blind? Might he not have resort to the law and see every word and sentence in it when he pleased? And what could he mean by those wondrous things? Were they the wonderful stories of the creation, the deluge, and Israel's passing through the Red sea, and the like? Were not his eyes open to read these strange things when he would? Doubtless by wondrous things in God's law, he had respect to those distinguishing and wonderful excellencies, and marvellous manifestations of the divine perfections and glory, contained in the commands and doctrines of the word, and those works and counsels of God that were there revealed. So the Scripture speaks of a knowledge of God's dispensation and covenant of mercy and way of grace towards his people, as peculiar to the saints, and given only by God,

Psalm 25:14. "The secret of the Lord is with them that fear him; and he will show them his covenant."

And that a true and saving belief of the truth of religion is that which arises from such a discovery, is also what the Scripture teaches. As John 6:40. "And this is the will of him that sent me, that every one who seeth the Son, and believeth on him, may have everlasting life;" where it is plain that a true faith is what arises from a spiritual sight of Christ. And, John 17:6, 7, 8. "I have manifested thy name unto the men which thou gavest me out of the world.—Now they have known that all things whatsoever thou has given me, are of thee. For I have given unto them the words which thou gavest me, and they have received them, and have known surely that I came out from thee, and they have believed that thou didst send me;" where Christ's manifesting God's name to the disciples, or giving them the knowledge of God, was that whereby they knew that Christ's doctrine was of God, and that Christ himself proceeded from him, and was sent by him. Again, John 12:44, 45, 46. "Jesus cried and said, He that believeth on me, believeth not on me, but on him that sent me. And he that seeth me, seeth him that sent me. I am come a light into the world, that whosoever believeth on me, should not abide in darkness." There believing in Christ, and spiritually seeing him, are parallel.

Christ condemns the Jews, that they did not know that he was the Messiah, and that his doctrine was true, from an inward distinguishing taste and relish of what was divine, in Luke 12:56, 57. He having there blamed the Jews, that though they could discern the face of the sky and of the earth, and signs of the weather, that they could not discern those times—or as it is expressed in Matthew, the signs of those times—adds, "yea, and why even of your own selves, judge ye not what is right?" *i.e.* without extrinsic signs. Why have ye not that sense of true excellency, whereby ye may distinguish that which is holy and divine? Why have ye not that savour of the things of God, by which you may see the distinguishing glory, and evident divinity, of me and my doctrine?

The apostle Peter mentions it as what gave him and his companions good and well-grounded assurance of the truth of the gospel, that they had seen the divine glory of Christ.—2 Peter 1:16. "For we have not followed cunningly devised fables, when we made known unto you the power and coming of our Lord Jesus Christ, but were eye-witnesses of his majesty." The apostle has respect to that visible glory of Christ which they saw in his transfiguration: that glory was so divine, having such an ineffable appearance and semblance of divine holiness, majesty, and grace, that it evidently denoted him to be a divine person. But if a sight of Christ's outward glory might give a rational assurance of his divinity, why may not an apprehension of his spiritual glory do so too? Doubtless Christ's spiritual glory is in itself as distinguishing, and as plainly shows his divinity, as his outward glory,— nay, a great deal more: for his spiritual glory is that wherein his divinity consists: and the outward glory of his transfiguration showed him to be divine, only as it was a remarkable image or representation of that spiritual glory. Doubtless, therefore, he that has had a clear sight of the spiritual glory of Christ, may say, I have not followed cunningly devised fables, but have been an eye-witness of his majesty, upon as good grounds as the apostle, when he had respect to the outward glory of Christ that he had seen. But this brings me to what was proposed next, *viz.* to show that,

Secondly, This doctrine is rational.

1. It is rational to suppose, that there is really such an excellency in divine things—so transcendent and exceedingly different from what is in other things—that, if it were seen, would most evidently distinguish them. We cannot rationally doubt but that things divine, which appertain to the Supreme Being, are vastly different from things that are human; that there is a high, glorious, and God-like excellency in them, that does most remarkably difference them from the things that are of men; insomuch that if the difference were but seen, it would have a convincing, satisfying influence upon any one, that they are divine. What reason can be offered against it? unless we would argue, that God is not remarkably distinguished in glory from men.

If Christ should now appear to any one as he did on the mount at his transfiguration; or if he should appear to the world in his heavenly glory, as he will do at the day of judgment; without doubt, his glory and majesty would be such as would satisfy every one, that he was a divine person, and that religion was true: and it would be a most reasonable and well-grounded conviction too. And why may there not be that stamp of divinity, or divine glory, on the word of God, on the scheme and doctrine of the gospel, that may be in like matter distinguishing and as rationally convincing, provided it be but seen? It is rational to suppose, that when God speaks to the world, there should be something in his word vastly different from men's word. Supposing that God never had spoken to the world, but we had notice that he was about to reveal himself from heaven, and speak to us immediately himself, or that he should give us a book of his own inditing; after what manner should we expect that he would speak? Would it not be rational to suppose, that his speech would be exceeding different from men's speech, that there should be such an excellency and sublimity in his word, such a stamp of wisdom, holiness, majesty, and other divine perfections, that the word of men, yea of the wisest of men, should appear mean and base in comparison of it? Doubtless it would be thought rational to expect this, and unreasonable to think otherwise. When a wise man speaks in the exercise of his wisdom, there is something in every thing he says, that is very distinguishable from the talk of a little child. So, without doubt, and much more, is the speech of God to be distinguished from that of the wisest of men; agreeable to Jeremiah 23:28, 29. God having there been reproving the false prophets that prophesied in his name, and pretended that what they spake was his word, when indeed it was their own word, says, "The prophet that hath a dream, let him tell a dream; and he that hath my word, let him speak my word faithfully: what is the chaff to the wheat? saith the Lord. Is not my word like as a fire? saith the Lord: and like a hammer that breaketh the rock in pieces."

2. If there be such a distinguishing excellency in divine things; it is rational to suppose that there may be such a thing as seeing it. What should hinder but that it may be seen? It is no argument, that there is no such distinguishing excellency, or that it cannot be seen, because some do not see it, though they may be discerning men in temporal matters. It is not rational to suppose, if there be any such excellency in divine things, that wicked men should see it. Is it rational to suppose, that those whose minds are full of spiritual pollution, and under the power of filthy lusts, should have any relish or sense of divine beauty or excellency; or that their minds should be susceptive of that light that is in its own nature so pure and heavenly? It need not seem at all strange, that sin should so blind the mind, seeing that men's particular natural tempers and dispositions will so much blind them in secular matters; as when men's natural temper is melancholy, jealous, fearful, proud, or the like.

3. It is rational to suppose, that this knowledge should be given immediately by God, and not be obtained by natural means. Upon what account should it seem unreasonable, that there should be any immediate communication between God and the creature? It is strange that men should make any matter of difficulty of it. Why should

not he that made all things, still have something immediately to do with the things that he has made? Where lies the great difficulty, if we own the being of a God, and that he created all things out of nothing, of allowing some immediate influence of God on the creation still? And if it be reasonable to suppose it with respect to any part of the creation, it is especially so with respect to reasonable intelligent creatures; who are next to God in the gradation of the different orders of beings, and whose business is most immediately with God; and reason teaches that man was made to serve and glorify his Creator. And if it be rational to suppose that God immediately communicates himself to man in any affair, it is in this. It is rational to suppose that God would reserve that knowledge and wisdom, which is of such a divine and excellent nature, to be bestowed immediately by himself; and that it should not be left in the power of second causes. Spiritual wisdom and grace is the highest and most excellent gift that ever God bestows on any creature: in this the highest excellency and perfection of a rational creature consists. It is also immensely the most important of all divine gifts: it is that wherein man's happiness consists, and on which his everlasting welfare depends. How rational is it to suppose that God, however he has left lower gifts to second causes, and in some sort in their power, yet should reserve this most excellent, divine, and important of all divine communications, in his own hands, to be bestowed immediately by himself, as a thing to great for second causes to be concerned in? It is rational to suppose, that this

blessing should be immediately from God, for there is
no gift or benefit that is in itself so nearly related to the
divine nature. Nothing which the creature receives is so
much a participation of the Deity: it is a kind of emanation of God's beauty, and is related to God as the light is
to the sun. It is therefore congruous and fit, that when it
is given of God, it should be immediately from himself,
and by himself, according to his own sovereign will.

It is rational to suppose, that it should be beyond
man's power to obtain this light by the mere strength of
natural reason; for it is not a thing that belongs to reason,
to see the beauty and loveliness of spiritual things; it is
not a speculative thing, but depends on the sense of the
heart. Reason indeed is necessary in order to it, as it is by
reason only that we are become the subjects of the means
of it; which means I have already shown to be necessary in
order to it, though they have no proper causal influence
in the affair. It is by reason that we become possessed of
a notion of those doctrines that are the subject-matter
of this divine light, or knowledge; and reason may many
ways be indirectly and remotely an advantage to it. Reason
has also to do in the acts that are immediately consequent
on this discovery: for seeing the truth of religion from
hence, is by reason; though it be but by one step, and
the inference be immediate. So reason has to do in that
accepting of and trusting in Christ, *that* is consequent
on it. But if we take *reason* strictly—not for the faculty
of mental perception in general, but for ratiocination,
or a power of inferring by arguments—the perceiving

of spiritual beauty and excellency no more belongs to reason, that it belongs to the sense of feeling to perceive colours, or to the power of seeing to perceive the sweetness of food. It is out of reason's province to perceive the beauty or loveliness of any thing: such a perception does not belong to that faculty. Reason's work is to perceive truth and not excellency. It is not ratiocination that gives men the perception of the beauty and amiableness of a countenance, though it may be many ways indirectly an advantage to it; yet it is no more reason that immediately perceives it, than it is reason that perceives the sweetness of honey: it depends on the sense of the heart.—Reason may determine that a countenance is beautiful to others, it may determine that honey is sweet to others; but it will never give me a perception of its sweetness.

I will conclude with a very brief improvement of what has been said.

First, This doctrine may lead us to reflect on the goodness of God, that has so ordered it, that a saving evidence of the truth of the gospel is such, as it is attainable by persons of mean capacities and advantages, as well as those that are of the greatest parts and learning. If the evidence of the gospel depended only on history, and such reasonings as learned men only are capable of, it would be above the reach of far the greatest part of mankind. But persons with an ordinary degree of knowledge are capable, without a long and subtle train of reasoning, to see the divine excellency of the things of religion: they are capable of being taught by the Spirit of God, as well as learned men. The evidence that is this way obtained, is vastly better and more satisfying, than all that can be obtained by the arguings of those that are most learned, and greatest masters of reason. And babes are as capable of knowing these things, as the wise and prudent; and they are often hid from these when they are revealed to those. 1 Corinthians 1:26, 27. "For ye see your calling, brethren, how that not many wise men after the flesh, not many mighty, not many noble, are called. But God hath chosen the foolish things of the world—."

Secondly, This doctrine may well put us upon examining ourselves, whether we have ever had this divine light let into our souls. If there be such a thing, doubtless it is of great importance whether we have thus been taught by the Spirit of God; whether the light of the glorious gospel of Christ, who is the image of God, hath shined unto us, giving us the light of the knowledge of the glory of God in the face of Jesus Christ; whether we have seen the Son, and believed on him, or have that faith of gospel-doctrines which arises from a spiritual sight of Christ.

Thirdly, All may hence be exhorted, earnestly to seek this spiritual light. To influence and move to it, the following things may be considered.

1. This is the most excellent and divine wisdom that any creature is capable of. It is more excellent than any human learning; it is far more excellent than all the knowledge of the greatest philosophers or statesmen. Yea, the least glimpse of the glory of God in the face of Christ doth more exalt and ennoble the soul, than all

the knowledge of those that have the greatest speculative understanding in divinity without grace. This knowledge has the most noble object that can be, *viz.* the divine glory and excellency of God and Christ. The knowledge of these objects is that wherein consists the most excellent knowledge of the angels, yea, of God himself.

2. This knowledge is that which is above all others sweet and joyful. Men have a great deal of pleasure in human knowledge, in studies of natural things; but this is nothing to that joy which arises from this divine light shining into the soul. This light gives a view of those things that are immensely the most exquisitely beautiful, and capable of delighting the eye of the understanding. This spiritual light is the dawning of the light of glory in the heart. There is nothing so powerful as this to support persons in affliction, and to give the mind peace and brightness in this stormy and dark world.

3. This light is such as effectually influences the inclination, and changes the nature of the soul. It assimilates our nature to the divine nature, and changes the soul into an image of the same glory that is beheld. 2 Corinthians 3:18. "But we all with open face, beholding as in a glass the glory of the Lord, are changed into the same image, from glory to glory, even as by the Spirit of the Lord." This knowledge will wean from the world, and raise the inclination to heavenly things. It will turn the heart to God as the fountain of good, and to choose him for the only portion. This light, and this only, will bring the soul to a saving close with Christ. It conforms the heart to the

gospel, mortifies its enmity and opposition against the scheme of salvation therein revealed: it causes the heart to embrace the joyful tidings, and entirely to adhere to, and acquiesce in the revelation of Christ as our Saviour: it causes the whole soul to accord and symphonize with it, admitting it with entire credit and respect, cleaving to it with full inclination and affection; and it effectually disposes the soul to give up itself entirely to Christ.

4. This light, and this only, has its fruit in an universal holiness of life. No merely notional or speculative understanding of the doctrines of religion will ever bring to this. But this light, as it reaches the bottom of the heart, and changes the nature, so it will effectually dispose to an universal obedience. It shows God as worthy to be obeyed and served. It draws forth the heart in a sincere love to God, which is the only principle of a true, gracious, and universal obedience; and it convinces of the reality of those glorious rewards that God has promised to them that obey him.

NOTES

NOTES

NOTES

MAN'S QUESTIONS & GOD'S ANSWERS

Am I accountable to God?
"Every one of us shall give account of himself to God." (Romans 14:12).

Has God seen all my ways?
"All things are naked and opened unto the eyes of Him with whom we have to do." (Hebrews 4:13).

Does He charge me with sin?
"The Scripture hath concluded all under sin." (Galatians 3:22).
"All have sinned." (Romans 3:23).

Will He punish sin?
"The soul that sinneth, it shall die." (Ezekiel 18:4).
"For the wages of sin is death." (Romans 6:23).

Must I perish?
"God is not willing that any perish, but that all should come to repentance." (2 Peter 3:9).

How can I escape?
"Believe on the Lord Jesus Christ, and thou shalt be saved." (Acts 16:31).

Is He able to save me?
"He is able also to save them to the uttermost that come unto God by Him." (Hebrews 7:25).

Is He willing?
"Christ Jesus came into the world to save sinners." (1 Timothy 1:15).

Am I saved on believing?
"He that believeth on the Son hath everlasting life." (John 3:36).

Can I be saved now?
"Now is the accepted time; behold, now is the day of salvation." (2 Corinthians 6:2).

As I am?
"Him that cometh to Me I will in no wise cast out." (John 6:37).

Shall I not fall away?
"Him that is able to keep you from falling." (Jude 24).

If saved, how should I live?
"They which live should not henceforth live unto themselves, but unto Him which died for them." (2 Corinthians 5:15).

What about death, and eternity?
"I go to prepare a place for you; that where I am, there ye may be also." (John 14:2, 3).

Made in the USA
Monee, IL
14 October 2022

15867041R00025